Billie
the Hippo

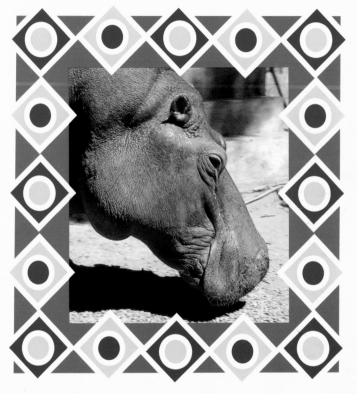

by Donna Malane
photographs by Cam Feast

Learning Media®

Contents

1. Who Is Billie?

"**H**ippopotamus" is a very big name for a very big animal. Most people just call it a "hippo."

Billie the hippo lives with Sheila, but Billie isn't really a pet.

Hippos are sometimes called the wildest animals in Africa. But Billie isn't really a wild animal, either.

Billie is like a pet because she lives with people. But she's still a wild animal because she's too big for a person to control properly.

Billie's head is huge. She has a big mouth, with teeth so long they are like **tusks**.

Billie has a body that is shaped like a **barrel**.

Billie's skin looks like the tires on a car.

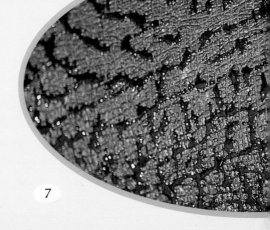

Billie has very short legs, but you would be surprised at how fast she can run. A hippo can run up to thirty miles per hour. That's as fast as cars drive around town.

Each foot has four toes with very thick toenails. Imagine having to cut those toenails!

Billie weighs one and a half tons.

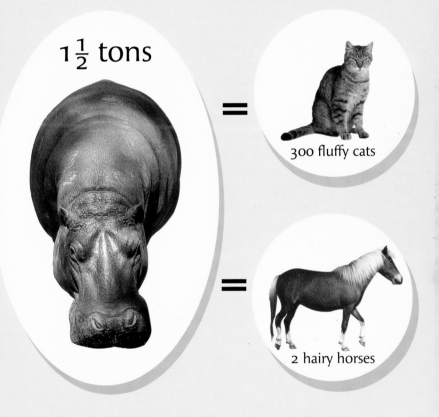

$1\frac{1}{2}$ tons

= 300 fluffy cats

= 2 hairy horses

How many children would it take to equal Billie's weight?

2. Billie in the Bathtub

Billie lives right beside the Kafue River in Zambia, Africa.

Like all hippos, she needs to lie in water that covers her skin so that she won't get sunburned.

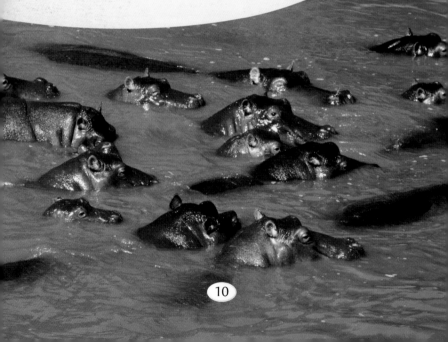

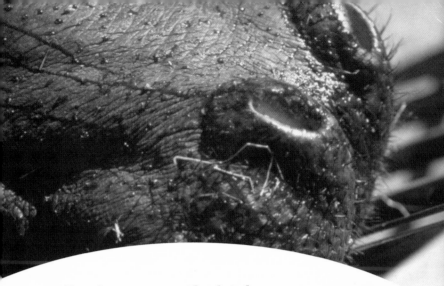

Billie has **nostrils** high up on her **muzzle**.

She can lie underwater for a very long time with just the top of her head poking out. Her big nostrils mean that she can take very deep breaths.

Billie has her own special bathtub. She is happy to lie in it for hours and hours.

Now that Billie has grown up, she's nearly too big for her bathtub. Imagine growing so big that you couldn't fit into your bathtub!

Billie eats mostly grass. She has to **graze** a lot to get enough to eat. Billie eats about thirty pounds of food a day. That's the same as sixty really big burgers!

Billie stays close to water as she grazes so that she can lie in it if she needs to.

3. Animal Family

Billie lives at an animal **orphanage** called Chimfunshi, in Zambia. This is where Sheila works.

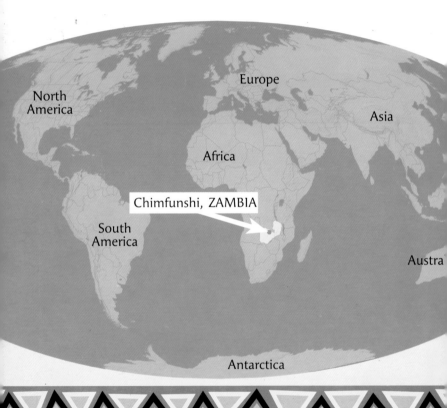

North America

Europe

Asia

Africa

Chimfunshi, ZAMBIA

South America

Austra

Antarctica

People bring all kinds of animals to Chimfunshi for Sheila to look after. Billie was one of these animals.

Sheila also looks after nearly one hundred chimpanzees. The chimpanzees were orphans when they came to live at Chimfunshi. Sheila and the other animals became their new family.

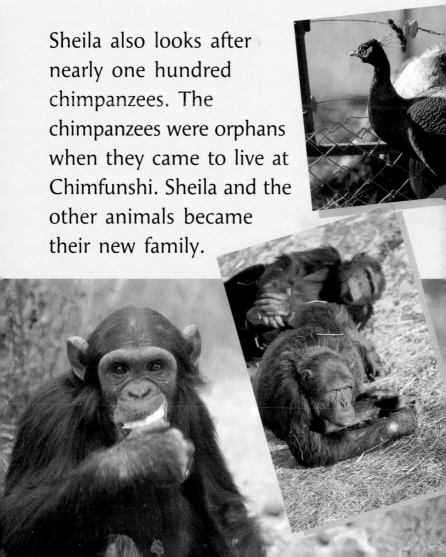

4. Baby Billie

Where did Billie come from? Well, she was only three days old when she was found by some **local** people. Her mother had been killed, and she was all alone. Billie was brought to the orphanage. Sheila became Billie's mother.

Sheila made bottles of milk for Billie to drink. At first, Billie wouldn't drink them. But she soon learned that Sheila was her new mother.

Then she drank three HUGE bottles of milk – every day!

Sheila would lie down beside Billie
each night so that Billie wouldn't be
too lonely.

Once Billie was used to Sheila,
she followed her everywhere.

At night, Billie would come into
Sheila's house, lie on the sofa,
and watch TV.

Soon, Billie grew too big to lie on the sofa. She had to lie on the floor instead. Then Billie grew too big for the floor!

Whenever Billie turned around in Sheila's house, she knocked something over, like a chair or a houseplant. Sheila decided that Billie was too big to come inside her house. Billie had to stay outside.

Billie is now eight years old. She would still like to come into Sheila's house, but she can't fit through the door. When she tries to come in, the whole house shakes!

5. Billie, Big and Strong

Billie loves to be near people because she has been part of Sheila's family since she was a baby.

Billie doesn't realize how strong she really is.

Once, she turned her big head so fast that she knocked Sheila over and broke her wrist.

Sheila knows that Billie didn't mean to hurt her, but now she's careful whenever she's near Billie.

Billie has started to wander off on her own. Sometimes, she's away for nearly two weeks.

Sheila thinks that Billie goes away to be with other hippos. Hippos usually live in a **herd**. They like to be with their family and friends – just like people do.

When Billie is gone, Sheila looks up the Kafue River. She hopes to see Billie in the river or to see her grazing with other hippos on the wide, grassy **plains**. Sheila hopes that Billie is learning how to be friends with the other hippos.

6. Happy Hippo

Even though Billie goes away, she always comes back home to Sheila.

Billie still thinks that Sheila is her mother. Billie still seems happy to be Sheila's baby.

Sheila hopes that one day Billie will have a baby hippo of her own. If she does, do you think that Billie will try to bring her baby inside to watch TV?